• STEPHANIE M

Are you ready to *meet your person?*

How to prepare your heart for the day your love story begins

Copyright © 2020 by Stephanie May Wilson
StephanieMayWilson.com
All rights reserved.

No part of this publication may be reproduced, stored in a retrieval system, or transmitted in any form or by any means, electronic, mechanical, photocopying, recording, scanning, or otherwise, without the prior written permission of the author, except in the case of brief quotations embodied in critical articles or reviews.

This publication is designed to provide accurate and authoritative information in regard to the subject matter covered. It is sold with the understanding that neither the author nor the publisher is engaged in rendering legal, investment, accounting or other professional services. While the publisher and author have used their best efforts in preparing this book, they make no representations or warranties with respect to the accuracy or completeness of the contents of this book and specifically disclaim any implied warranties of merchantability or fitness for a particular purpose. No warranty may be created or extended by sales representatives or written sales materials. The advice and strategies contained herein may not be suitable for your situation. You should consult with a professional when appropriate. Neither the publisher nor the author shall be liable for any loss of profit or any other commercial damages, including but not limited to special, incidental, consequential, personal, or other damages.

Are You Ready to Meet Your Person?
How to Prepare Your Heart for the Day Your Love Story Begins
By Stephanie May Wilson

RELIGION / Christian Life / Love & Marriage

ISBN: 978-1-7348715-0-0

Holy Bible, New International Version®, NIV®
Copyright ©1973, 1978, 1984, 2011 by Biblica, Inc.®
Used by permission. All rights reserved worldwide.

Design by Luum Studio
HelloLuum.com

Printed in the United States of America

//
Are You Ready To Meet Your Person?

Introduction

I always thought I'd have some warning before my single life was about to end.

I thought I'd have a gut feeling, or a dream a few months out. Maybe it'd be like having a baby: You'd find out nine months ahead of time that your future husband was on the way, and then you'd have those nine months to get things in order. You could check a few more things off your bucket list, get your heart ready, pray a little extra, and maybe start eating a few more vegetables.

But that's not how it happened for me.

I'd just moved my whole life from Colorado to Georgia for a new job at a mission organization. It was my first day of work, and I was a total ball of nerves.

Is my outfit okay? Am I making a good first impression? What was that form I was supposed to bring with me? What is my new boss's name again?

I was thinking about a lot of things on that day, but truly, the very last thing on my mind was the idea that I might meet my future husband.

But that's exactly what happened.

My new boss guided me around the office on that first day, introducing me to the team. "This is Emily," he said. "She's the copywriter for the marketing department."

INTRODUCTION

Then, turning his attention to the desk next to Emily's, he said, "And this is our creative director, Carl Wilson."

And just like that, my single life was over. The train left the station. I'd met my future husband.

Now, to be fair, it took us about a month to realize we liked each other, and we dated for a while before we realized we wanted to marry each other. But that process—the process of meeting Carl, getting to know him, discovering that he was my person, and getting married—started on that very day.

And I am so glad I was ready. Because if it had happened just a few years (or even months!) earlier, I wouldn't have been.

What It Means To Be Ready

Everyone will define this differently, and the truth is that, in some ways, marriage is like having kids. I'm not sure you're ever really ready, because you're stepping into something you've never done before!

But the thing I've come to understand is that there are some key areas of growth, where if we work through these things before we meet our person, it will make the dating process, engagement, and marriage so much easier.

I had to figure these things out the hard way in my own life.

The truth is, my single life wasn't always smooth sailing. I had so many hard moments along the way—times when I got it wrong, got rejected, or wondered, *why hasn't this happened for me yet?* There were years of my life when (I hate to admit this!) I idolized marriage and looked at singleness as something I had to endure before I got to the good part of life. I wanted to close my eyes, hunker down, and wait it out until it was finally over and my life could officially begin.

Luckily, I had some wonderful friends and mentors who stepped in along the way.

They helped me see that singleness isn't a waiting room for marriage, it's an important, wonderful, fun season of our lives. It's a season to be savored, enjoyed, and invested in. They helped me see that if I were to invest in myself while I was single, it would not only make that season of my life so much better, but it would also make a huge difference in my future marriage—transforming my marriage before it even started.

I took their advice and decided that if I had this time of being single, I might as well make the most of it, and that decision changed my life.

Today, when I look back on that time, I remember it so fondly. I wouldn't take back a minute of it. It was wild, transformative, and so much fun.

Not only that, but it's precisely because of how I invested in my single life that I was ready to meet my future husband when I did.

It's because of these very things that I was in the right place at the right time as the best version of myself to meet Carl, and to catch his eye.

But the impact didn't stop there.

It's because of those things—the learning, growing, investing, and becoming — that our marriage is as sweet and wonderful as it is today. We're five years in, and we grow more and more in love each day. And so much of that is that's because of the decisions we made before we even met each other.

And here's the best part: the things I did are totally repeatable for you. The very first step to make this your story too is to work through this reflection guide!

So, are you ready to get started?

How To Use This Guide

There are eight reflection questions in the guide. Some of them are longer, some are shorter, some might feel easy to answer, and some might take a bit more time. I made sure to give you plenty of room to write, so feel free to answer each question with as much detail as you'd like.

Quick note: If you're reading this digitally, you'll need a piece of paper, a journal, or a spot on your phone where you can record your answers.

If you can, try to give yourself at least an hour to work through this. That might be more time than you need, but I don't want you to feel rushed. Find a place that's quiet, free of interruptions, and comfortable. Put on your favorite pair of sweatpants, pour yourself a cup of tea or make yourself a snack, and settle in.

If your mind is feeling particularly busy right now, spend some time reading and relaxing before you get started. Pick up a devotional or a book you love. Read a few pages of something that will help your heartbeat slow, your mind clear, and your body relax enough so you can hear from yourself.

OH, AND LET'S TALK ABOUT THE ANSWER KEY...

On the last several pages, you'll find the answer key. (Don't cheat and go there first!) After you answer the questions, the answer key will have an explanation to go along with each one, telling you why I asked the question and how to interpret your answer.

Are you ready? Let's dive in...

Imagine the day you meet your future husband. Picture the scene. Where are you? What are you doing? What is your first interaction like? Once you have a few of those details sketched out in your mind, move your attention to yourself. Who are you on the day you meet your husband? What qualities and characteristics are true about you? What does your life look like? Jot down a few of the things that come to mind and then take a few minutes to reflect. Are there any things that you want to be true about you then that aren't true about you now?

QUESTION 1

ARE YOU READY TO MEET YOUR PERSON?

QUESTION 1

Question 2

Which words more accurately describe how you feel about your overall life in this season: Joy and contentment? Or dissatisfaction and frustration?

QUESTION 2

ARE YOU READY TO MEET YOUR PERSON?

QUESTION 2

Question 3

If you were on a first date and the guy asked you, "Tell me about yourself! What does your life look like these days?" Do you feel like you'd have a lot to say? Are you proud of the life you'd get to tell him about?

QUESTION 3

ARE YOU READY TO MEET YOUR PERSON?

QUESTION 3

Question 4

Do you feel comfortable and confident in your own skin? Do you like the person you are today?

QUESTION 4

ARE YOU READY TO MEET YOUR PERSON?

QUESTION 4

Question 5

What does your relationship with God look like today? Do you feel close to Him? Do you feel like you have a thriving spiritual life?

QUESTION 5

ARE YOU READY TO MEET YOUR PERSON?

QUESTION 5

Question 6

If you were to start planning a wedding tomorrow, do you know who your bridesmaids would be? Do you have a good support system of friends surrounding you?

QUESTION 6

ARE YOU READY TO MEET YOUR PERSON?

QUESTION 6

Question 7

We all have hard things that happen to us throughout life. Is there anything in your life that's been particularly hard that you might not have worked through yet? (A big loss, something traumatic, a past relationship, something within your family, etc.)

QUESTION 7

ARE YOU READY TO MEET YOUR PERSON?

QUESTION 7

Question 8

Do you know what you're looking for in a relationship? Do you know what qualities you're hoping to find in a future husband?

QUESTION 8

ARE YOU READY TO MEET YOUR PERSON?

QUESTION 8

Answer Key

Now that you've taken the time to answer those questions, let's talk through them together! For each one, I'm going to share with you why I asked the question and what your different answers might say about whether or not you're ready to meet your person.

When you reach the end, you might consider bringing your workbook and your answers to a trusted friend, mentor, pastor, or counselor. They know you and know where you are in life right now, and they'll be able to talk through your answers with you and give you some personalized insight.

Question 1

Imagine the day you meet your future husband. Picture the scene. Where are you? What are you doing? What is your first interaction like? Once you have a few of those details sketched out in your mind, move your attention to yourself. Who are you on the day you meet your husband? What qualities and characteristics are true about you? What does your life look like? Jot down a few of the things that come to mind and then take a few minutes to reflect. Are there any things that you want to be true about you then that aren't true about you now?

A mentor asked me this question just a few years before I met my husband. I had been lamenting the fact that I really thought I was ready to meet my person, but he just hadn't shown up in my life yet. That's when she hit me with it....

"Who do you want to be on the day you meet your husband? Are there any things that you want to be true about you then that aren't true about you now?"

For years, I had thought I was ready. I felt ready. My heart felt ready. And by that, I mean that my heart often ached with how much I wanted to meet my person and get married.

But when she asked me this question, and when I really took the time to answer it, I was surprised by the truth: maybe I wasn't so ready after all.

I wanted to be the best version of myself on the day I met my future husband—full of joy and confidence. I wanted to have a rich, fulfilling life to

ANSWER KEY: QUESTION 1

invite him into, a great group of friends, and a deep, connected relationship with God. I wanted to have healed from some of the things I'd been through over the last several years so I wouldn't bring that baggage into our marriage.

As I reflected on her question, and on my life as it was that day, I could see that there was a bit of a gap between those two people—the person I was at the time, and the person I wanted to be when my future husband walked into my life.

I realized I had some room to grow. My mentor helped me see that if I did that growing, the marriage I'd end up with would be so much better as a result.

And she was right.

So, friend, as you reflect on your answer to Question #1, what do you think? Are you who you hope to be on the day you meet your person? Or, are you having the same realization I did? Are there a few changes you want to make before that day comes?

Either answer is okay and wonderful. The most important thing is that you're taking the time to answer the question. The fact that you're thinking through this today means you're committed to being thoughtful and intentional with both this season and the next, and that'll make all the difference.

Question 2

Which words more accurately describe how you feel about your overall life these days: Joy and contentment? Or dissatisfaction and frustration?

The reason I ask this question, and what I want you to be on the lookout for is if you're hoping a relationship will fix something in you or your life. That's a warning sign that you might not be ready. While marriage adds so much to our lives, it will never fix our lives. It was never supposed to.

If we're looking to another person to fix us or a part of our lives, that often has a few different results:

1. It causes us to settle for people who might not be right for us. (A lot of really unhealthy relationships start this way!)

2. It leaves us feeling dissatisfied and disappointed when the relationship doesn't come through as the fix we were hoping it would be. (This is the cause of a lot of unhappiness in marriages.)

3. It impairs our ability to be the healthy partner our person deserves.

4. It puts too much pressure on the relationship and on the other person, which can lead to fighting, resentment, and alienation.

Now, keep in mind, we have all done this. We have all looked to a relationship to fix a whole host of problems in our lives.

ANSWER KEY: QUESTION 2

So if you're doing this right now, know that you're not alone!

But you should also know that there's a better way—a way that leads to healthier relationships and a healthier you:

If you have some areas of your life where you're feeling particularly frustrated or dissatisfied, the best thing you can do is to take some time to work on those things directly.

Here's an example of this from my life:

For me, one of the hardest parts about being single was the loneliness that sometimes crept in.

There were days as a single person when the loneliness was palpable—when I could feel my heart aching for the person I hoped to share my life with someday.

It was extra tough anytime I'd look around and find myself surrounded by happy couples. It felt like everyone else had their person, their built-in best friend, someone to support them, help them, do life with them, and simply love them. It felt like everyone else had someone to go home with, and there I was, driving home alone.

In seasons when this was particularly tough for me, I'd find myself looking over at people in relationships thinking that they were so lucky because they didn't have to feel lonely anymore.

I found myself believing that if I could just get married, any feelings of loneliness, isolation, or lack would go away.

But, just a few years later, I found out that I was wrong.

I found out that romantic relationships don't cure our loneliness. It just doesn't work that way.

The weekend before our wedding, my husband Carl and I moved from Georgia to Tennessee. We moved to Nashville, a town where I didn't know one single person but him.

That was the beginning of the loneliest season of my life.

I cried every single day for months because I was so lonely, and it had nothing to do with Carl. He was (and is!) an amazing husband. Our connection is so deep and good and rich and warm. I wasn't lonely for him; I was lonely for everyone else!

I've learned so much about relationships over the years, and when I think about our relational lives, I always picture a pie graph (remember those from math class?). Our heart has different parts to it that all long for different types of connection. And unfortunately (or fortunately!) romantic relationships don't satisfy every piece of that pie.

Even though he's an amazing husband, Carl doesn't replace my need for girlfriends. He can't replace my need for a good and deep connection with my family. Him loving me can't overcome the loneliness I might feel in my own skin by not being in a good relationship with myself. His wisdom and insight can't replace that of a counselor or a mentor—I need those too. And he absolutely cannot replace the loneliness of being disconnected from God.

Friend, I believe with my whole heart that if you want to, you will get married someday. And I know he'll be incredible, and your marriage will be fantastic, and that part of your heart will feel so warm and connected. But I also know that you could get married to this amazing guy, and still feel lonely. We need more than just this relationship in our lives.

ANSWER KEY: QUESTION 2

But here's the good news. While you can't control the timing of this handsome man showing up on the scene, you can work on the other parts of your life in the meantime!

So that's my challenge for you today. If you've identified some areas of your life that you've been hoping a relationship will fix (like I was with loneliness!), take some time to brainstorm how you might be able to work on those things today—before your person enters the picture. Start investing in yourself, your relationship with God, in your family, and your friends. Start investing in your healing, and your growth, and your development as a person.

And here's the thing, if you do this, if you seek healing, fulfillment, and completeness from the right sources in your life, you'll be free to step into marriage without putting so much pressure on your spouse. You'll be able to find someone really great and be really great for them—it'll set you up for a healthy, happy life together.

You can do this, and both your life and your future marriage will be so much better as a result!

Question 3

If you were on a first date and the guy asked you, "Tell me about yourself! What does your life look like these days?" Do you feel like you'd have a lot to say? Are you proud of the life you'd get to tell him about?

Back in high school, when I was applying for colleges, I had a meeting with our school's college counselor. I knew which colleges I wanted to get into, and I wanted any help I could get in making my applications the best they could be.

I was a fairly good student, was involved in all kinds of sports and activities at my school, and I felt like I was a strong candidate for the schools I had my eye on.

I felt confident as I sat across from the college counselor. Without any pleasantries or small talk, he sat back in his chair and said, "So, tell me about yourself." And with that, my confidence disappeared in a flash.

I faltered. I wasn't expecting that. What did he want to know? Anything? Everything? I didn't know where to start.

So, I started listing off my accomplishments. "This is my GPA, I'm involved in these activities, I have this letter of recommendation..." (My confidence was returning.)

Now, I don't think he actually rolled his eyes, but that was definitely the vibe I was getting from him as he leaned across his desk toward me.

ANSWER KEY: QUESTION 3

"Stephanie, every single student applying to these schools has that exact same list of accomplishments. What makes you stand out? What makes you an interesting person?"

I responded like a deer in the headlights—my eyes wide, my mind a total blank.

What made me an interesting person? I had absolutely no idea.

Now, the end of this story is that I got accepted to some of the colleges and rejected by others. And I can't remember if I ever saw that college counselor again. But that one interaction was enough to stick with me forever.

To be fair, it wasn't the kindest question, or the gentlest way of asking it. But it was a good question, and an important one that we need to answer.

What made me interesting? What makes us interesting?

This question, and the answers people are looking for, differ a bit when we're talking about first dates instead of college applications, but the principle is still helpful.

When you're on a first date, and the person across from you says, "Tell me about yourself!", what do you have to say? Are you proud of the things you have to say?

Can you tell them about the trip you took recently with your best friend, about the Spanish class you take on Saturday mornings, or about the team you volunteer with at church?

Or, will you only be able to tell them about the latest Netflix show you binge watched?

Now, I love Netflix as much as anybody. But the first answers are, frankly, more interesting and compelling than the second. That's how we'd see it if we were the ones asking the questions!

My mom and dad have been married for almost 40 years and even though they've been married for most of their lives, at least once a month my dad tells a story that my mom has never heard before. We'll be at dinner when he'll come out with a story from one of the first jobs he ever had, a prank he pulled on his brother, or something that happened when he was in the military. And my mom will shake her head and laugh as she says "I swear, just when I think I know all of his stories, there's another one I haven't heard before!"

They've been married for 40 years and are still getting to know each other, and it's because they're both interesting people with deep wells of experiences, thoughts, and stories for the other to explore and get to know.

Someone recently asked Carl how he and I prepared for marriage, and the advice he gave was remarkably similar to the advice from that college counselor. He said, "Become an interesting person. Live a full life today so you have something wonderful to invite someone into."

And I just love that.

This season of your life, right now, is the season when you get to live the stories you'll be sharing for the rest of your life. This is the season when you get to become the person your future person will marry.

Fortunately, and unfortunately, we don't change all at once when we meet our person or when we walk down the aisle.

ANSWER KEY: QUESTION 3

You'll wake up the day after your wedding still being you—with all of your gifts, strengths, stories, and experiences; with all of your bad habits, quirks, and the areas where you're still trying to grow.

And so if you can use this season while you're single to really become the best, most interesting version of yourself, and to live the best, most fulfilling life possible, not only will that give you some wonderful things to talk about over dinner on that very first date, but you'll have a rich life to invite this person into—which will make your marriage so much better for decades to come.

If you're sitting here thinking, "Steph, I feel like I'm living a really wonderful, full life," then my friend, I'm cheering you on. The fact that you're doing that will probably be the way you meet the great person you're looking for! It'll be something about you that totally captivates them, and it'll set you up for a wonderful marriage in the future.

But if you're sitting here thinking, "Honestly, I don't know how I'd answer that question. My life doesn't feel full, or fun, or interesting at all." Friend, you're so not alone.

So many of us find ourselves in that place, and it's actually a lot easier to get out of than we sometimes imagine.

Here's a great first step: Do one thing this week that scares you. Just one. It can be signing up for a new workout class or reading a book that you thought was a bit over your head. It can be inviting a friend to coffee or going to an event at your church. Do one thing this week that scares you. That's a great step in the right direction.

(Note: If you could use some extra help in this area, I have a resource I'd love to share with you! Head over to DoubleYourDatingProspects.com to hear all about it.)

Question 4

Do you feel comfortable and confident in your own skin? Do you like the person you are today?

Shortly after I graduated from college, I started dating a great new guy. He liked me a lot and I liked him a lot. There was just one big problem in our relationship: I didn't like me.

Maybe that sounds silly, and you're wondering, "Why would that even matter?" Or maybe you're thinking, "You had this great guy dating you, how could you still not like yourself?" But I'm telling you, I really didn't.

I was drowning in insecurity and nothing he did helped. It didn't matter how well he treated me, how many dates he took me on, what he said to me, or how many times he sent me flowers. It was never enough to make me feel better about myself.

It wasn't the whole reason we broke up, but it was definitely part of it. And this was a huge wake-up call for me.

I always thought that if someone loved you, it would make it easier to love yourself. Or that maybe if they loved you, you wouldn't need to love yourself—their love would overpower all of your insecurity.

But I discovered that's just not true.

ANSWER KEY: QUESTION 4

If we don't have a good relationship with ourselves, if we see ourselves as totally, completely unlovable, it's really hard for anyone (even a wonderful guy!) to talk us out of it. Our sense of identity, confidence, and worth can't come from someone else. It has to come from within, and more than that, it has to come from God.

I worked on this for a long time in between that relationship and when I met my husband. I invested in my relationship with myself, learned a lot about God's love for me, and really worked on finding my identity in Him.

And I'll say, while I definitely still have days where I feel insecure, it is so much better now. My relationship with myself is so much better, and my relationship with my husband is so much better as a result.

I'm not smothering our relationship by looking to Carl to love me enough for the both of us. I'm not putting too much pressure on our marriage, hoping it fills a hole only God can fill. When Carl says, "I love you," I really believe him. I can receive his love because I feel worthy of love. And because I'm in a healthy place in my own life, I'm able to give that love right back.

So, friend, today I invite you to take a few minutes to examine how you're feeling about yourself. Remember that marriage isn't meant to fix the holes in our hearts. So if this is a hole that feels particularly deep for you, it's worth addressing before you jump into a relationship. But know that this investment in yourself will make your future relationships so much better.

And if you are feeling comfortable, confident, and secure in your identity (most of the time, anyway), then you might really be ready to meet your person!

Question 5

What does your relationship with God look like today? Do you feel close to Him? Do you feel like you have a thriving spiritual life?

When I dreamed about my future relationships and future marriage, there was one prayer that always topped the list. I wanted to marry someone who loves God. I wanted our marriage to be a godly one. The problem is, I think we have some misconceptions about what a godly marriage looks like and how we go about cultivating one.

What I've come to understand is that a godly marriage isn't just two people who read a devotional together sometimes once they're married. A godly marriage is when two people who deeply love God decide to love Him together. And the great news is, you have half of that equation long before you have a clue who your husband might be!

I cannot say this enough: the very best thing that I did while I was single was to invest deeply in my relationship with God. It truly changed everything for me.

When God swooped into my life, He brought redemption, meaning, joy, and a fresh start. God has helped me make incredible friends, pursue my dreams, and feel beautiful, like I'm enough in my own skin. He brought me into an adventurous, purpose-filled life that has been wilder and more wonderful than anything I ever could have dreamed. And those adventures are the reason I was in the right place at the right time to meet my sweet husband.

ANSWER KEY: QUESTION 5

God is deeply woven into the fabric of my life and Carl's life, and because of that, our marriage together has been richer and more wonderful than I ever could have imagined.

And so, friend, if faith is really important to you, if you want to be in a relationship with someone whose faith is really important to them, and if you want to have God at the center of your relationship, then it's so important that you invite God into the center of your life today.

Oh, and that's another thing we tend to forget about . . .

So many of us would say that we're looking for a guy who's really strong in his faith, but we need to remember that a guy who is strong in his faith is looking for a girl who is too!

We need to be the kind of person we want to be with.

So, take some time to think through your relationship with God as it stands today. Are you where you want to be in your faith when you meet your future person?

One last thing to keep in mind: Friend, this does not have to be perfect. If you're sitting there thinking that you have to miraculously transform into the perfect Christian before you'll be ready to get married, let me take that pressure off you right this second.

There's no such thing as a perfect Christian. If we could be perfect, we wouldn't need Jesus. So please don't let that pressure hold you back. The important thing is that if your faith deeply matters to you, then prioritize it in your life—do what you can do to love God more, to get closer to Him, and to become more like Him each and every day.

That's the very best thing you can do to prepare your heart to meet your person.

Question 6

If you were to start planning a wedding tomorrow, do you know who your bridesmaids would be? Do you have a good support system of friends surrounding you?

Let me start this by saying that you don't need to know who your bridesmaids will be before you meet your future husband. This is just a question to get you thinking about the support system you have in your life right now, and the support system you hope to have when it's time for you to get married.

Carl and I got married on a beautiful summer evening a few years ago, and while my favorite moment of the weekend was the, you know, getting married part, my other favorite moment of the weekend happened during our rehearsal dinner.

Carl isn't a frequent crier. Although I've seen him tear up on several occasions, I'd never seen him really cry until this point. At our rehearsal dinner, he stood in front of our family and friends and gave a toast to my bridesmaids. He cried the whole way through, thanking them for making me the woman I am today. The night before we got married, he made a point to recognize the women who have impacted me more deeply, more permanently than anyone else in my life.

Suffice it to say he wasn't the only one crying as he made that toast.

Friend, we need each other—a group of women to cook with, go out with, laugh with, and do nothing with.

ANSWER KEY: QUESTION 6

We need women who will bring us dinner when something bad happens or answer our call at 4:00 a.m. to pray with us or tell us it's going to be okay. We need women who tell us the truth and shake us out of our mess when we need a strong word from someone who truly knows us. We need each other. We need a team in our corner. We need people who are our people.

We especially need each other as we navigate relationships.

Relationships are one of the most beautiful, most important, and most gut-wrenching parts of our lives. Romance is the area where our brains seem to shut down, and our hearts seem to go into overdrive. In other words, we could use some help. And that's exactly why we need a team of girlfriends by our side and in our corner.

I'm not sure I would have survived my single and dating life without my girlfriends. (It certainly wouldn't have been as much fun without them!) My girlfriends were the ones to tell me the honest truth when a guy wasn't treating me the way I deserved. They were the ones who helped me pick up the pieces in the wake of my most heart-wrenching breakups. They were the ones who helped me choose an outfit for a first date, and they were the first ones I told when a guy named Carl had asked me out.

Not only were they instrumental in my dating life, they've helped me in my marriage so much as well. They're my sounding board, our support system. They've helped me navigate all the wonderfully strange things that come when you combine your life with a boy—from setting up your first place, and merging your finances, to sex and what it means to be a good wife.

That's what bridesmaids are there for. They stand next to you at your wedding and promise to help you along the way. Their presence in your wedding is a vow that they're on your team as you two get married. You don't have to figure this out alone.

(Let's be honest, they're not up there for the dresses!)

Take a few minutes to look back over your answer. Do you have a lot of friends right now or are you in a season when you're wishing for more, or deeper, friendships?

If you find that you have great friendships, I'm so happy for you! These friendships will help you so much in life and in your relationships. They might be how you meet your person; they'll be the ones who cheer you on along the way, and they'll be the ones who stand next to you as you say, "I do."

But maybe these great friendships sound more like a dream than a reality for you right now. Maybe you look around your life and feel really lonely. Maybe you just moved to a new city or your friends just moved away (or got married or had a baby, which sometimes can feel like the same thing). Maybe you're feeling distant from the people who used to be your people, or maybe you feel like you never quite found your people.

If you're in this place right now, please know that you're not alone. I know it seems like everyone already has their best friends, but I promise you that's not true. So many women feel lonely and disconnected. You're not alone in feeling this way!

But here's what you need to know today: It's never too late to start a new chapter in your friendship story. It's never too late to find your best friend, to find your people. It takes some time and some intentionality. But you can do it, and I promise, it's worth it.

Question 7

We all have hard things that happen to us throughout life. Is there anything in your life that's been particularly hard that you might not have worked through yet? (A big loss, something traumatic, a past relationship, something within your family, etc.)

Life can be so hard sometimes, can't it? Throughout our lives, we all go through things that wound us, break us, and totally knock us over.

I have conversations all the time with women who have been in abusive relationships, who have suffered at the hands of family members, whose parents are in the middle of a divorce, or who are in the middle of a divorce themselves. I have girlfriends who are grieving a big loss—some are grieving the loss of a job or a dream, others are grieving the loss of a loved one. And the list goes on and on. (I so wish this wasn't happening to our friends and sisters!)

Every single one of us experiences heartbreak, trauma, and really hard things as we walk through life on this beautiful but broken earth. And while these things don't discount us from love (not at all!) it is important that we take the time to heal.

Because often, our unhealed hurts lead us into unhealthy relationships.

Here are a few examples:

A few years ago, a dear friend of mine found herself in a manipulative and emotionally abusive relationship. It was terrible. He was a truly unhealthy person, and we were thrilled when she ended the relationship for good.

But not long after she got out of that relationship, she hopped into another one. She didn't take the time to heal, process, or get counseling (which is really what she needed), and the saddest thing is that the next guy she dated could have been the first guy's twin.

This unhealed hurt turned into a pattern in her life, and became difficult to break.

Another friend of mine is weathering her parents' divorce. Her dad was unfaithful to her mom, which has torn her family apart.

My friend started dating a wonderful guy in the midst of this season, but much to both of their frustrations, she found herself totally unable to trust him.

He did nothing wrong and nothing to lose her trust. But because of what her parents were going through, and because she didn't have time to process and heal from her father's betrayal, she was projecting all of that mistrust onto a guy who didn't deserve it.

A reader of mine reached out to me after the death of her beloved grandfather. They were so close—best friends, really—and his death completely broke her heart.

A few days after the funeral, she was out with some friends when a guy approached their table. He thought she was cute, asked for her number, and they started to date. She told me that her friends could see immediately that he wasn't a good guy, but she was so blinded by grief and so desperate for distraction and comfort, she wasn't able to see how unhealthy the relationship was.

She said, "I stayed in that terrible relationship for a year. It was such a mistake. I wish I had just healed from my loss and then started dating. My grief really impaired my judgment."

Friend, if you're in the midst of a tough season right now, or if something sad, painful, or traumatic has happened in your past, it's really important that you take the time to deal with it and heal from it.

I know this is so hard (I'm with you!), but doing this work will make a world of difference in your life today and in your marriage down the road.

On the other hand, if you have already done this work, or if nothing is coming to mind, that's great, and it really might mean that you're ready.

Question 8

Do you know what you're looking for in a relationship? Do you know what qualities you're hoping to find in a future husband?

What are some qualities that you are really hoping to find in your future husband? Kindness, strength, courage, integrity? A sense of humor, a love for adventure, a passion for family? Marriage is a life-changing decision, and it's important to know what you're looking for.

But I think when we consider our must-have lists of what's important to us, we tend to swing in one of two directions, and they can both get us into trouble.

One mistake so many of us make is that we don't really have a must-have list. We want to be in a good relationship and that's about all we know. But we've never taken the time to define "good"— to define what we're looking for.

That lack of clarity leaves us out in the dating wilderness without a map. We try dating one guy, and when that doesn't work out, we try someone else. We ping-pong through different relationships and get our hearts broken into pieces along the way.

This can also lead us to settle for the wrong guy. How can you possibly know if he's wrong if you've never defined what's right? This scenario is so hard because marriage is one of the only things in our lives that is totally un-doable. I guess divorce is technically an option, but divorce leaves us broken and battered, and it rips apart families.

ANSWER KEY: QUESTION 8

There's no way to painlessly slip out of a marriage, so it's really important that we get this right.

The other extreme is that sometimes our must-have lists are way too specific. Our expectations are so high, our mile-long list of requirements blinds us to so many great men out there!

There was a time when I thought I could not possibly marry someone who wasn't six foot two, blond, and a youth pastor. But if I had kept my list this specific, I would have missed out on meeting Carl—an amazing man who is not blond or a youth pastor, but who is absolutely perfect for me.

What we're looking for here is a happy medium.

We need to have a filter so we can date with intentionality and purpose and so we don't end up doing a lot of avoidable trial and error and getting our hearts broken forty-seven times along the way. (Or worse, settling for someone who doesn't treat us the way we deserve to be treated!)

But we also need to open up our hands, our plans, and our criteria so there's room for God to know better than we do.

We need to be open-minded enough to go on a date with the guy who intrigues us, but who we're not totally sure about, because that guy may just end up being the one. And we never would have known that if we wrote him off right away for having the "wrong" hair color or having the "wrong" career.

So, friend, with all of this in mind, take another look at your answer to Question #8. Do you feel like you have a good grasp on what kind of person you're looking for? Have you taken the time to think through this, to learn from your past relationships, and to intentionally look ahead? Do you need some time to think this through before you put yourself back out there?

Or, is your list so long that it's actually keeping you from meeting some really great guys (and potentially meeting your husband!)? If so, it might be time to narrow it down to the things that are truly most important, and let God surprise you with the rest!

You did it!

You finished the reflection guide! How did it go?

Take a few minutes to reflect in the space below. After answering all of these questions, and after reading through the answer key, do you feel like you're ready to meet your person? Or are there some areas of your life that you might want to invest in today so you can bring your very best self into your marriage down the road?

YOU DID IT!

ARE YOU READY TO MEET YOUR PERSON?

YOU DID IT!

One Last Thing

When thinking about the future and reflecting on the past, it's easy to be so hard on ourselves. We're mad at ourselves for that one mistake we made a few years ago. We're frustrated that we haven't made more progress lately. We're angry at ourselves for not yet being where we want to be. But friend, you have come so far. You have persevered through so much, and you are in the process of growing—right now, today.

So, for our last exercise, I invite you to spend a few minutes reflecting on those truths, and then, in the space below, write yourself a letter of encouragement. You are so worthy of love, my friend, and you're worthy of your own love too.

ONE LAST THING

ARE YOU READY TO MEET YOUR PERSON?

ONE LAST THING

Thank You

Thank you so much for joining me for this reflection guide! I'm so honored to have gotten to share it with you.

Whether you've discovered you're ready or that you need a little bit more time before your person comes along, I hope you feel proud of yourself today.

You put time and effort into this guide, and that shows that you're approaching your life with intentionality. That intentionality will help you so much in your journey as an individual and in your future marriage.

There are such good things ahead for you, and I'm cheering you on like crazy as you step into them.

All my love,

Stephanie

P.S. Make sure to keep reading. I have a little gift for you!

Next Steps

Whether you've decided, "Yes! I'm ready to meet my person!" or "Nope, I need a little bit more time to work on myself and my life before I add another person into it," you may be wondering, "What do I do next?"

If you've discovered that you are ready to meet your person, you might find yourself wondering:

So, why hasn't it happened yet?

How do I find this person?

Should I put myself out there more?

Should I practice patience and wait on God?

What does waiting on God actually look like?

And when I do meet someone who I think might be someone special, what do I do then?

Do I wait for him to make the first move?

Do I guard my heart? What does guarding your heart even mean?

NEXT STEPS

It seems like the second we decide we're ready to meet our person, our minds are flooded with 8,000 questions about what we should do next. (Or was that just me?)

Or you might be sitting here thinking, "I'm not quite ready to meet my person," which leaves you wondering, "How do I get myself to a place where I am ready?"

You might be asking:

How do I heal the parts of my heart that feel a bit broken right now?

How can I feel more content in my life so I don't put too much pressure on a relationship?

How do I get to a place where I feel more confident and sure of my identity in Christ?

How do I get closer to God?

Where do I find that group of girlfriends who will walk with me through this?

How do I get my heart ready for a relationship?

How do I live the kind of life that I'm excited to invite someone into?

These are all such good questions, and I have a resource that can help with all of them!

It's a guided prayer journal called *Every Single Moment: 100 Powerful Prayers to help you Savor the Present and Prepare for the Future*.

ARE YOU READY TO MEET YOUR PERSON?

Filled with easy-to-follow prayer prompts, this beautiful 100-day guided journal is designed to help you cover your future husband and marriage in prayer.

But that's just the beginning...

Over the course of 100 days, these prayer prompts will help you heal from the past, grow in the present, and find joy, peace, and purpose in your life right now, today.

You'll feel connected with God through prayer in a whole new way—leaving you full of joy, alive with hope, and ready for love.

Best of all, when you finish the journal, you'll find yourself with a beautiful time-capsule keepsake of this chapter of your love story, and where God showed up in the midst of it.

Every Single Moment really is a life-changing way of praying for your future husband, and starting on the next page, you'll find seven of my favorite prompts from the journal so you can try it out and see if it might be a helpful next step for you.

So, are you ready? Here's a sneak peek of my 100-day guided prayer journal, *Every Single Moment*.

Every Single Moment

Dear Friend,

I started my very first journal in sixth grade. I had a new boyfriend named Erik, and I was entirely unsure how I felt about him (I mean, you remember sixth grade, right?). I purchased a small black journal with matte black pages, and in silver gel pen, I began pouring out everything I was thinking and feeling.

That journal started something very real and incredibly important in my life, and I've been journaling ever since—recording, day-by-day, the first, slightly sloppy draft of the story of my life.

I became a Christian at the end of college. That's when someone told me you could journal and pray at the same time; that writing your prayers to God was not only a way to keep your mind from wandering, but also a great way to keep a record of God's faithfulness in your life. It made perfect sense to me, and it fit how I already processed thoughts and emotions. Needless to say, I jumped on that train immediately. Fast forward nearly a decade and I have boxes and boxes of prayer journals. They're my most prized possession.

One of my favorite prayer journals is the one I kept in the season just before I met my husband, Carl. I was ready to meet my person, and it was painful watching so many of my friends meet their husbands first. It was a lonely season for me in a lot of ways, but it was also a rich, transformative, and wildly fun time in my life as well—and to be honest, I'm not sure if I would have noticed that without this habit of prayer journaling.

INTRODUCTION

I was praying about a lot of things in those days—pouring out pages and pages of hopes, dreams, and fears. I was praying that God would help me become the woman He created me to be, and that He would use me to do big and beautiful things in the world. I was praying about my identity and my friendships, both of which felt a bit rocky in those days, and I wanted to see growth and change. I wanted to savor these days and to make the most of every single moment of this season of my life. In the midst of all of that, I was also praying for my future husband and for the life we'd build together.

Every single one of those prayers made a difference in my life back then and in my marriage today. Through them, God helped me heal from the past, live in the present, and prepare for the future in the most beautiful way.

Prayer journaling plays a central role in my life and I recommend it to everyone I meet—especially people navigating singleness, dating, and all the feelings this season brings with it.

A prayer journal invites you to peek into your heart, gather up what you find, and sort through it with God's help. As you open up these tender parts of yourself to God, He steps into them and changes you, redeems you, heals you, and transforms you in ways you might not even be able to imagine.

Prayer journals are also a great way to document your story as it's happening. Our lives go by quickly, and if you're anything like me, you can't even remember what you ate for dinner last week, let alone details that happened months or even years ago. I love having a record of what I was doing just weeks before I met my husband. I love re-reading my thoughts from the moments just before our first date. I love reading the prayers I was praying for our future marriage and seeing all the ways they've been answered.

Our journals are the first draft of our life story—our love story.

They're a gift to our future selves, a beautiful keepsake documenting God's presence and faithfulness in our lives. That's what I pray this journal becomes for you.

I'm also praying that this prayer journal brings you peace.

The thing most people gloss over is the fact that prayer is hard. It's like folding a fitted sheet— we're never sure if we're doing it right. Prayer for your future person is even harder. There may be times when you don't pray into your future because you're not sure if it matters. I'm here to tell you that it does matter! After all, deciding who to marry will impact your life more than any other decision. You definitely want God to be a part of it. But sometimes, the opposite is true, and you might find yourself only praying about your future husband, idolizing both him and marriage. Prayer becomes a way to feel like you're living in a future that you haven't reached quite yet. When your focus is solely on the future, you risk missing out on the present, and it is actually living and praying in the present that will prepare you for that glowing future you dream of.

I created this prayer journal to help with the journey. It's a guide to help you make the most of every single moment by savoring the present, which is the very best way to prepare for your future life, your future marriage, and your future family. Best of all, this is a keepsake—a record of your story and the loving God who showed up in the midst of it. So, let's begin. Are you ready?

Pray that God would help you as you begin this prayer journey. Ask Him to help you be brave and bold and intentional with the next one hundred days. Ask Him to help you do the things you know you need to do to become the woman you want to be. Ask Him to meet you in the midst of this adventure, to answer your prayers, and to transform both you and your life along the way.

Know that I'll be praying for you the whole way through.

All my love,

Stephanie

Day 1

There's nothing you can do to make God love you more than He does right now, and there's nothing you can do to make God love you less than He does right this second. Because of Jesus, you're in good standing with God. He loves you, you have access to Him, and He wants a relationship with you—right this second, and forever. Take some time to journal about how it feels to hear that truth today.

DAY 1

EVERY SINGLE MOMENT

DAY 1

How are you feeling about your current relationship status—your love life as it is today? Are you feeling lonely or impatient or frustrated? Are you hurting or anxious? Maybe you're feeling content right now. Whatever you're feeling is totally fine (and totally normal!). Practice honesty with God as you tell Him about this today. He's in this with you. You don't have to walk through this alone!

DAY 2

EVERY SINGLE MOMENT

DAY 2

When all of your girlfriends, siblings, and Facebook friends seem to be getting married at the same time, it's easy to feel like you're falling behind in life (which of course puts a ton of pressure on every date and takes all the fun out of it). But friend, I promise you're not. You're not falling behind, you're not falling short, and you haven't missed your chance. God is writing a beautiful story in your life, and the timing will be perfect.

Proverbs 3:5 says, "Trust in the Lord with all your heart," (NIV) but that's easier said than done—especially when you're trying to muster up the faith and patience on your own! Take a few minutes to pray for His perfect help as you learn to trust God's perfect timing.

DAY 3

EVERY SINGLE MOMENT

DAY 3

Day 4

Insecurity has the power to absolutely cripple your love life. It's hard to accept and reciprocate someone's love when you don't think you're worthy of it. And it's impossible to put yourself out there when you think no one will ever choose you.

Friend, when you look at your love life—past and present, and when you think about what the future may hold—can you see any ways in which insecurity may be holding you back? Do you think your love life could be better if you felt more confident and more worthy of love? Reflect on that with God today. Ask Him to fill you up with the truth of how loved and how worthy of love you truly are.

DAY 4

EVERY SINGLE MOMENT

DAY 4

Spend a few minutes reflecting on how you've been showing up for your life. Have you been an active participant in your love life? Have you been intentionally working towards the future you're hoping for? Or are you hanging back, hoping God plops the right guy on your front doorstep? (Like I did for so long!)

Write two or three things that have been holding you back, and then ask God to help you break through those barriers so you can begin taking the big steps that only you can take toward the life and the relationship of your dreams.

DAY 5

EVERY SINGLE MOMENT

DAY 5

What are some things you want to be true about your future marriage? If you aren't sure where to start, try thinking about it this way: When people interact with you and your husband, what do you want them to say about the way you love each other? Take some time to make a list and then pray for those things today.

DAY 6

EVERY SINGLE MOMENT

DAY 6

Take the next few minutes to pray for your future husband—wherever he might be. Pray for his heart, for his faith, for the things that might be happening in his life right now, and whatever else comes to mind! Pray that he's using this season before he meets you to grow, to heal, and to become the very best version of himself, knowing that his life today and your future marriage will be so much better as a result.

DAY 7

EVERY SINGLE MOMENT

DAY 7

That's the end of the sneak peek of *Every Single Moment*,
but this is just the beginning!

If you head to SMayWilsonShop.com/EverySingleMoment you can pick up
a copy of *Every Single Moment* and dive into the prayer journal today!

And, as a special gift, I have a discount code just for you. If you use the promo
code AREYOUREADY at checkout, it'll give you 15% off.

About The Author

Stephanie May Wilson is an author, a podcaster, a speaker, and the go-to guide for 20 & 30-something women as they navigate their most important relationships. Through her books, her courses, and her chart-topping podcast, "Girls Night," Stephanie has mentored more than a million women as they cultivate healthy, thriving relationships with God, their friends, their significant others, and with themselves.

Stephanie's writing has been featured on NBC, the Anthropologie blog, and Relevant Magazine, and she's been a long-time blog contributor for CNBC's Nightly Business Report, Darling Magazine, and the Christian Mingle blog.

When she's not writing, speaking, or recording a podcast episode, you can find Stephanie packing for a global adventure with her husband Carl, laughing with her close tribe of girlfriends, or snuggled up in yoga pants in her Nashville home.

Also by Stephanie May Wilson

Every Single Moment
100 Powerful Prayers to Savor the Present & Prepare for The Future

Love Your Single Life
Transform Your Season of Waiting into a Season of Passion, Purpose, and Preparation
- An Online Course -

Double Your Dating Prospects
A Step-by-Step Plan to Help You Put Yourself Out There
- An Online Course -

The Lipstick Gospel
A Story About Finding God in Heartbreak, the Sistine Chapel, and the Perfect Cappuccino

The Lipstick Gospel Devotional
90 Days of Saying Yes to a God Who Is Anything But Boring

Available at StephanieMayWilson.com.